I0521575

Year / Dates:

_____

This book belongs to:

_____

If lost, contact:

_____

Copyright © 2022 by Kathy Oneto.

All rights reserved. No part of this publication may be repro-
duced, distributed, or transmitted in any form or by any means,
including photocopying, recording, or other electronic or me-
chanical methods, without the prior written permission of the
publisher, except in the case of brief quotations embodied in
critical reviews and certain other non-commercial uses permit-
ted by copyright law. For permission requests, write to the au-
thor, at: kathyoneto@sustainableambition.com.

Kathy Oneto

Sustainable Ambition Press

https://SustainableAmbition.com

My Little Book of Curiosity / Kathy Oneto—1st ed.

Paperback ISBN 979-8-9853093-3-1
Hardcover ISBN 979-8-9853093-4-8

My Little Book of Curiosity

26 Inquiries to Inspire

What's Next for Your Life+Work

SUSTAINABLE AMBITION™

*"The greatest virtue of man
is perhaps curiosity."*

ANATOLE FRANCE

Contents

"What you seek is seeking you."

———

RUMI

Why *My Little Book of Curiosity?*

Hi there! Welcome to *My Little Book of Curiosity*, a learning exploration to uncover what might be next for your life+work.

What got you curious to open me? It might be that you've been pondering, "What do I want to do next?" And you find yourself saying, "I don't know!" You aren't alone. Yet, you are the only one who will know. The answers lie within you.

It takes getting quiet and hearing yourself to find the spark of insight. What you may have found is thinking hard about the answer doesn't make it materialize. What if you were to turn the experience of searching into one of exploration and wonder rather than hard work?

That's where *My Little Book of Curiosity* can help. I give you space to explore and to allow your mind to wander, seeing what catches your attention over time. What are you curious about? What are signals that give you insight on where you might want to go next?

And even if you aren't searching, paying attention to what you're curious about can help keep you on a growth and learning journey throughout your life and career. It's a good practice to start and keep from decade to decade.

Ready to get started? Let's dive into how it works.

"Mere curiosity adds wings to every step."

JOHANN WOLFGANG VON GOETHE

ADDITIONAL RESOURCES

Learn more about Sustainable Ambition at:
SustainableAmbition.com

Want to explore your curiosities with others? Find a guide to host a What's Next Curiosity Circle, along with other resources, at: SustainableAmbition.com/curiosity

It may feel like it, but there's no rush to find what's next. Rather, what works is slowing down time and creating space to hear yourself. So, keep me around and within reach to keep notes over a week, one month, three months, a year. You pick the time horizon.

There are 26 inquiries in Section 1 that provide you the opportunity to explore and wonder. Consider answering the inquiries during set times for journaling. Create a practice each morning, afternoon, or evening for a week or month and spend 15 minutes answering a few prompts and capturing whatever comes to your mind that day. You can also capture insights and ideas when they pop up. That's a reason to keep me close by.

Then every so often—at the end of a week or month or year—review the responses you've been creating. What patterns do you see emerging? There are pages in Section 2 where you can capture your reflections.

Now, don't forget about me! Keep your lists going and check in again over time. Are there any new patterns that start to emerge? Are themes converging?

At the end of the life of your book, summarize your overall observations and reflections. From what you've written and the themes, what might be next for you? Capture your insights in Section 3.

Sound fun? Sound illuminating? Let's go!

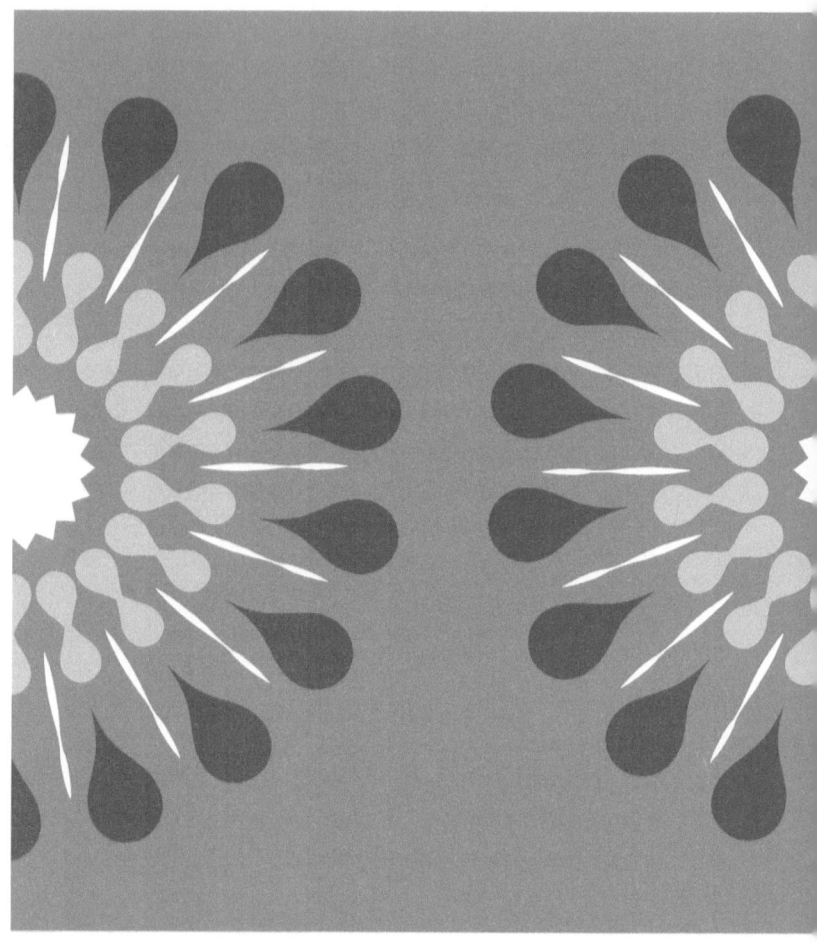

I am excited to explore...

_____

_____

_____

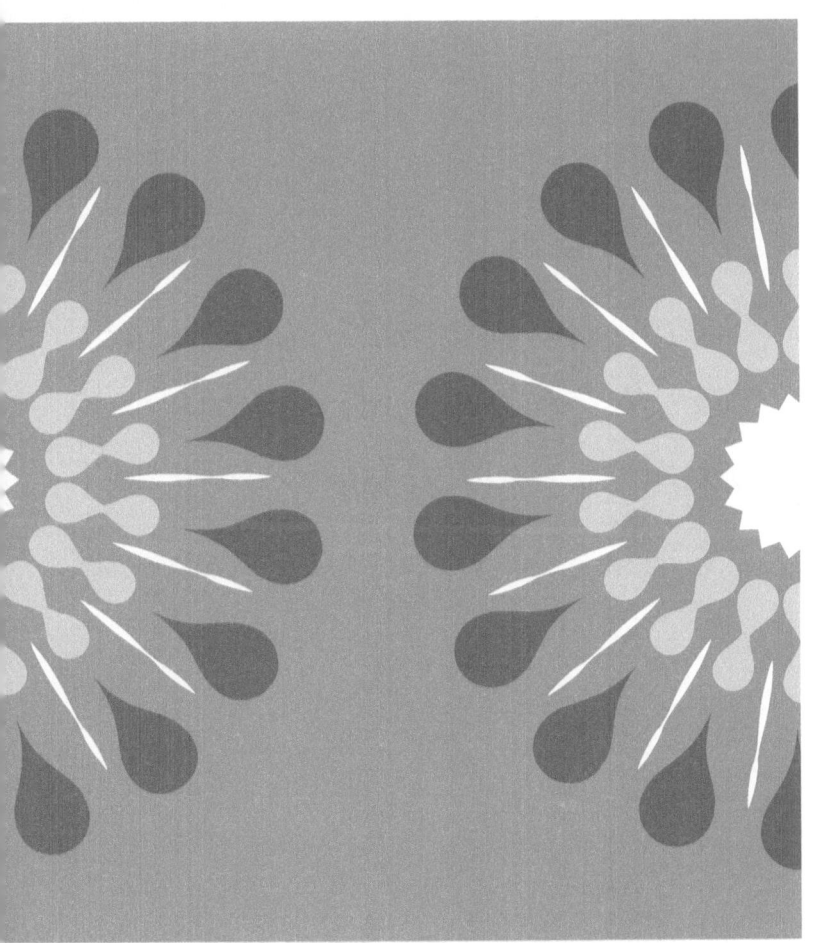

26 Inquiries
to Inspire What's Next

"What lies behind us and what lies before us are tiny matters compared to what lies within us."

RALPH WALDO EMERSON

Now it's time to diverge and explore.

Answer the inquiries that follow with free-flowing thought. Don't overthink your responses. There will be time to synthesize and analyze your responses later. For now, capture the ideas that pop into your mind. If you start a prompt and nothing flows to your fingertips, move on to another that inspires you.

Try one to three prompts at a time. Start with those that speak to you in the moment. It's okay to jump around. Consider creating a practice to answer the inquiries at a set time each day. Give yourself the gift of that time and space to let your mind wander and wonder.

Again, keep me close by to capture ideas when they come to you, so you can keep your lists active and living. And remember to not worry about finding an answer right now. There will be time to see the threads later.

Let the adventure begin!

1. Right now, I am curious about...

_____

_____

_____

_____

_____

_____

_____

_____

_____

_____

_____

_____

_____

_____

_____

_____

1. Right now, I am curious about...

_____

_____

_____

_____

_____

_____

_____

_____

_____

_____

_____

_____

_____

_____

_____

_____

_____

2. I'm drawn toward...

_____

_____

_____

_____

_____

_____

_____

_____

_____

_____

_____

_____

_____

_____

_____

_____

2. I'm drawn toward...

_____

_____

_____

_____

_____

_____

_____

_____

_____

_____

_____

_____

_____

_____

_____

_____

_____

3. What is calling me now is...

_____

_____

_____

_____

_____

_____

_____

_____

_____

_____

_____

_____

_____

_____

_____

3. What is calling me now is...

_____

_____

_____

_____

_____

_____

_____

_____

_____

_____

_____

_____

_____

_____

_____

_____

4. What is trending up for me is...

_____

_____

_____

_____

_____

_____

_____

_____

_____

_____

_____

_____

_____

_____

_____

_____

4. What is trending up for me is...

5. My attention is focused on...

---

5. My attention is focused on...

_____

_____

_____

_____

_____

_____

_____

_____

_____

_____

_____

_____

_____

_____

_____

_____

_____

6. I just can't stop thinking about...

_____

_____

_____

_____

_____

_____

_____

_____

_____

_____

_____

_____

_____

_____

_____

_____

6. I just can't stop thinking about...

_____

_____

_____

_____

_____

_____

_____

_____

_____

_____

_____

_____

_____

_____

_____

_____

7. I'd find it really interesting to (be/do)...

7. I'd find it really interesting to (be/do)...

_____

_____

_____

_____

_____

_____

_____

_____

_____

_____

_____

_____

_____

_____

_____

_____

_____

_____

8. I'm inspired by...

_____

_____

_____

_____

_____

_____

_____

_____

_____

_____

_____

_____

_____

_____

_____

_____

_____

8. I'm inspired by...

_____

_____

_____

_____

_____

_____

_____

_____

_____

_____

_____

_____

_____

_____

_____

_____

_____

_____

9. A goal that would be challenging, interesting, and hold my attention is...

_____

_____

_____

_____

_____

_____

_____

_____

_____

_____

_____

_____

_____

_____

_____

_____

9. A goal that would be challenging, interesting, and hold my attention is...

10. I'd like to have an impact on...

_____

_____

_____

_____

_____

_____

_____

_____

_____

_____

_____

_____

_____

_____

_____

_____

10. I'd like to have an impact on...

_____

_____

_____

_____

_____

_____

_____

_____

_____

_____

_____

_____

_____

_____

_____

_____

11. I'm really connected to and care about...

_____

_____

_____

_____

_____

_____

_____

_____

_____

_____

_____

_____

_____

_____

_____

_____

11. I'm really connected to and care about...

_____

_____

_____

_____

_____

_____

_____

_____

_____

_____

_____

_____

_____

_____

_____

_____

12. I want to contribute (to)....

_____

_____

_____

_____

_____

_____

_____

_____

_____

_____

_____

_____

_____

_____

_____

_____

_____

12. I want to contribute (to)....

_____

_____

_____

_____

_____

_____

_____

_____

_____

_____

_____

_____

_____

_____

_____

_____

_____

_____

13. I'd be disappointed if by the end of my life I didn't...

_____

_____

_____

_____

_____

_____

_____

_____

_____

_____

_____

_____

_____

_____

_____

_____

13. I'd be disappointed if by the end of my life I didn't...

_____

_____

_____

_____

_____

_____

_____

_____

_____

_____

_____

_____

_____

_____

_____

_____

_____

14. If I were to visit my future self, he/she/they would tell me to make sure I...

_____

_____

_____

_____

_____

_____

_____

_____

_____

_____

_____

_____

_____

_____

_____

_____

_____

14. If I were to visit my future self, he/she/they would tell me to make sure I...

_____

_____

_____

_____

_____

_____

_____

_____

_____

_____

_____

_____

_____

_____

_____

_____

_____

15. The way I'd really like to grow is...

_____

_____

_____

_____

_____

_____

_____

_____

_____

_____

_____

_____

_____

_____

_____

_____

_____

15. The way I'd really like to grow is...

_____

_____

_____

_____

_____

_____

_____

_____

_____

_____

_____

_____

_____

_____

_____

_____

_____

16. I would really like to learn...

_____

_____

_____

_____

_____

_____

_____

_____

_____

_____

_____

_____

_____

_____

_____

_____

16. I would really like to learn...

_____

_____

_____

_____

_____

_____

_____

_____

_____

_____

_____

_____

_____

_____

_____

_____

_____

_____

17. I would really like to try or practice...

_____

_____

_____

_____

_____

_____

_____

_____

_____

_____

_____

_____

_____

_____

_____

_____

17. I would really like to try or practice...

_____

_____

_____

_____

_____

_____

_____

_____

_____

_____

_____

_____

_____

_____

_____

_____

_____

_____

18. I really want to master...

_____

_____

_____

_____

_____

_____

_____

_____

_____

_____

_____

_____

_____

_____

_____

_____

_____

18. I really want to master...

_____

_____

_____

_____

_____

_____

_____

_____

_____

_____

_____

_____

_____

_____

_____

_____

_____

19. I love to do...

_____

_____

_____

_____

_____

_____

_____

_____

_____

_____

_____

_____

_____

_____

_____

_____

19. I love to do...

_____

_____

_____

_____

_____

_____

_____

_____

_____

_____

_____

_____

_____

_____

_____

_____

_____

20. What really brings me joy is...

_____

_____

_____

_____

_____

_____

_____

_____

_____

_____

_____

_____

_____

_____

_____

_____

_____

20. What really brings me joy is...

21. I feel alive when...

_____

_____

_____

_____

_____

_____

_____

_____

_____

_____

_____

_____

_____

_____

_____

_____

_____

21. I feel alive when...

_____

_____

_____

_____

_____

_____

_____

_____

_____

_____

_____

_____

_____

_____

_____

_____

22. My superpower is...

_____

_____

_____

_____

_____

_____

_____

_____

_____

_____

_____

_____

_____

_____

_____

22. My superpower is...

23. I'd love to be...

_____

_____

_____

_____

_____

_____

_____

_____

_____

_____

_____

_____

_____

_____

_____

_____

23. I'd love to be...

24. I want to build my identity around...

_____

_____

_____

_____

_____

_____

_____

_____

_____

_____

_____

_____

_____

_____

_____

_____

24. I want to build my identity around...

_____

_____

_____

_____

_____

_____

_____

_____

_____

_____

_____

_____

_____

_____

_____

_____

_____

_____

25. I'd like to build my character by...

_____

_____

_____

_____

_____

_____

_____

_____

_____

_____

_____

_____

_____

_____

_____

_____

_____

25. I'd like to build my character by...

_____

_____

_____

_____

_____

_____

_____

_____

_____

_____

_____

_____

_____

_____

_____

_____

_____

_____

26. I would like to become...

_____

_____

_____

_____

_____

_____

_____

_____

_____

_____

_____

_____

_____

_____

_____

_____

26. I would like to become...

_____

_____

_____

_____

_____

_____

_____

_____

_____

_____

_____

_____

_____

_____

_____

_____

_____

_____

_____

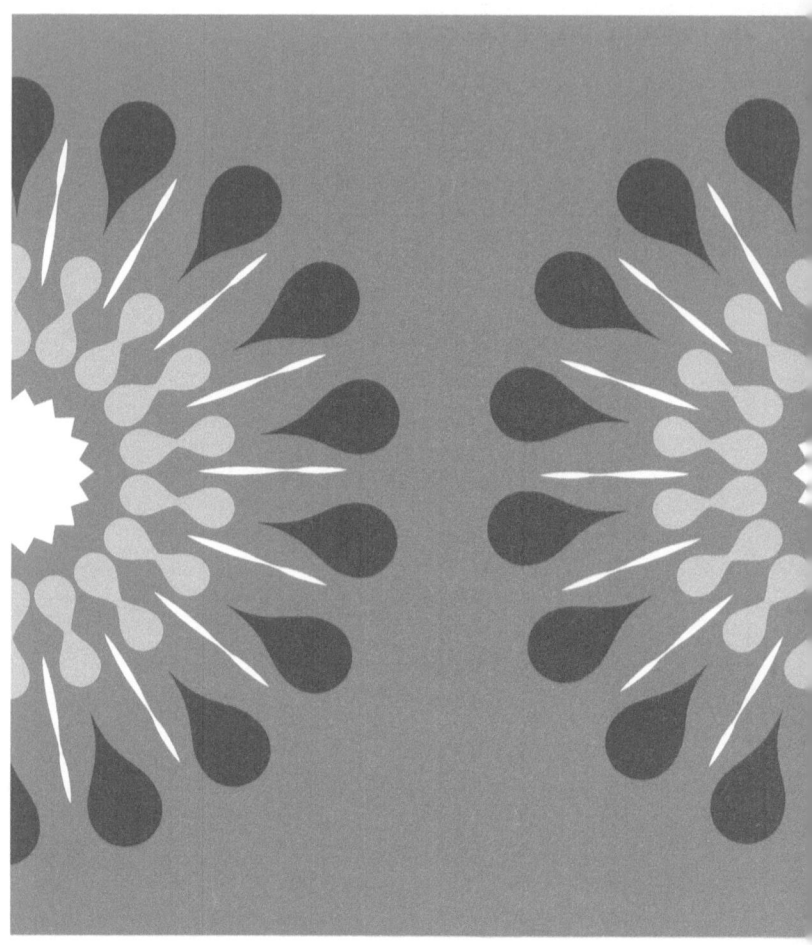

I am starting to see...

_____

_____

_____

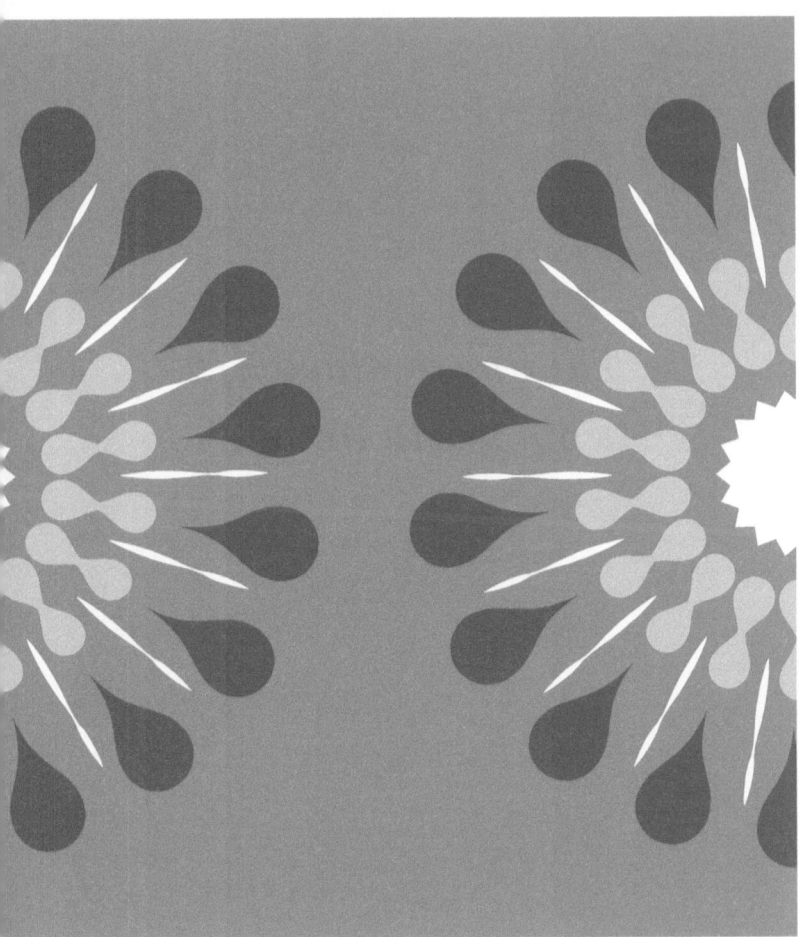

Find the Patterns

*"The unexamined life
is not worth living."*

———————

SOCRATES

Now it's time to converge. We often don't see patterns and can't connect the dots until we pause to look back and find the threads of consistency.

Look back to your lists periodically—after a week, perhaps a month, or when your responses are full—and use the next pages to note the themes that are emerging. Maybe you notice you're very curious about helping to empower young women in establishing a career in STEM. Or you wrote several times about wanting to start your own business or a non-profit. At times you may think the themes are generic but look closer. Often there are details one misses or skims over. Challenge yourself to see the nuance and specifics.

There are multiple pages to allow you to do this pattern-searching more than once over the course of the life of *My Little Book of Curiosity*. Each time you review your responses and find patterns, challenge yourself to take one action to test out a spark of insight and explore in some small way if a path might hold your interest and be what's next for you to explore either professionally or to bring into your personal life.

Ready, set, find the patterns!

Date: _____

Looking back at my lists, the themes emerging are...

_____

_____

_____

_____

_____

_____

_____

_____

_____

_____

One small action I'm going to take to further explore a spark is...

_____

_____

_____

Date: _____

Looking back at my lists, the themes emerging are...

_____
_____
_____
_____
_____
_____
_____
_____
_____
_____

One small action I'm going to take to further explore a spark is...

_____
_____
_____

PATTERNS

Date: _____

Looking back at my lists, the themes emerging are...

_____
_____
_____
_____
_____
_____
_____
_____
_____
_____
_____

One small action I'm going to take to further explore a spark is...

_____
_____
_____

Date: _____

Looking back at my lists, the themes emerging are...

_____

_____

_____

_____

_____

_____

_____

_____

_____

_____

One small action I'm going to take to further explore a spark is...

_____

_____

_____

Date: _____

Looking back at my lists, the themes emerging are...

_____

_____

_____

_____

_____

_____

_____

_____

_____

One small action I'm going to take to further explore a spark is...

_____

_____

_____

Date: _____

Looking back at my lists, the themes emerging are...

_____

_____

_____

_____

_____

_____

_____

_____

_____

_____

One small action I'm going to take to further explore a spark is...

_____

_____

_____

PATTERNS

Date: _____

Looking back at my lists, the themes emerging are...

_____

_____

_____

_____

_____

_____

_____

_____

_____

_____

One small action I'm going to take to further explore
a spark is...

_____

_____

_____

Date: _____

Looking back at my lists, the themes emerging are...

_____

_____

_____

_____

_____

_____

_____

_____

_____

_____

One small action I'm going to take to further explore a spark is...

_____

_____

_____

Date: _____

Looking back at my lists, the themes emerging are...

_____

_____

_____

_____

_____

_____

_____

_____

_____

_____

One small action I'm going to take to further explore a spark is...

_____

_____

_____

Date: _____

Looking back at my lists, the themes emerging are...

_____

_____

_____

_____

_____

_____

_____

_____

_____

_____

One small action I'm going to take to further explore a spark is...

_____

_____

_____

What's next for me is...

_____

_____

_____

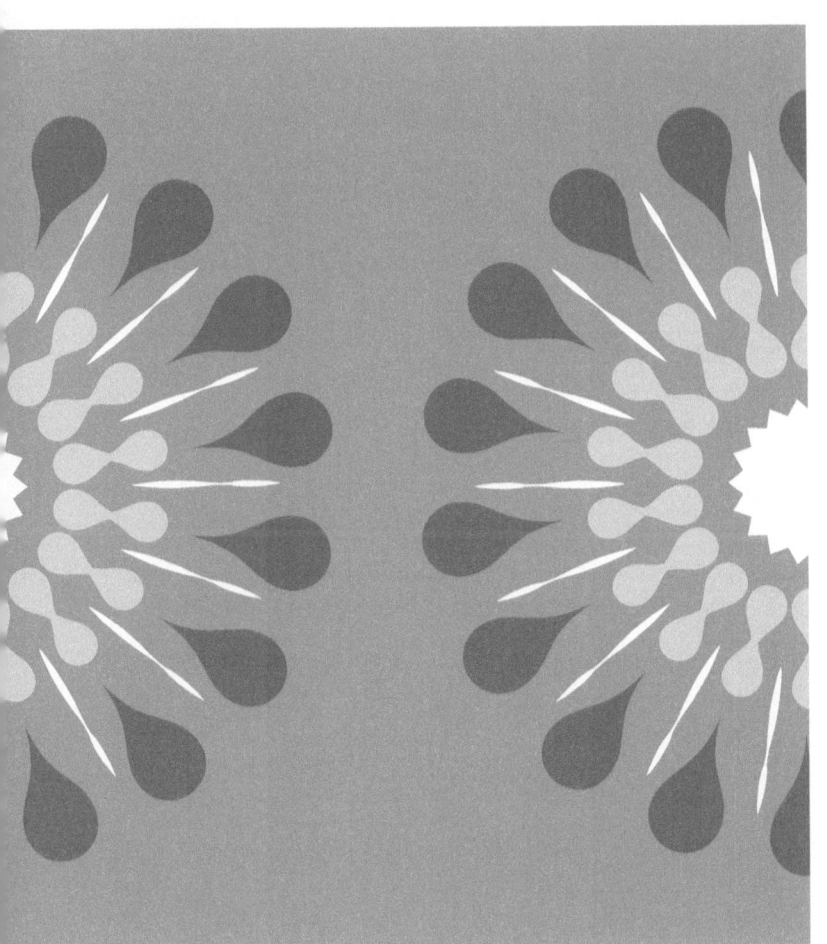

What's Next?

"Luck is what happens when preparation meets opportunity."

SENECA

*"Life is an unfoldment,
and the further we travel
the more truth we can comprehend."*

HYPATIA OF ALEXANDRIA

*"It is never too late to be
what you might have been."*

GEORGE ELIOT

Remember when you picked up this book and started out? You weren't sure what might be next for your life +work. And yet I told you that you were the only one who would know. You were the one who held the answer.

Now that you've spent time with the inquiries and finding patterns, you've given yourself the gift of space to explore and see what might be present for you. What sparks of insight showed up?

We often only get a glimmer of what we might want to do next, yet patterns are there. What did you find when you synthesized your responses and identified the threads?

At this stage, again carve out a little time and space to reflect and wonder. What's becoming clear for you around what's next?

What path do you want to start to put yourself on from here? What do you want to explore or experience further? What do you want to take action on?

Our lives and careers are a journey that can present different opportunities over time, while our work satisfaction and ambitions can ebb and flow from decade to decade. Paying attention and remaining curious is important to help keep you on a path of growth and learning and to build a sustainable, regenerative career.

So, keep up the practice! Stay curious!

What's next for me and the paths I'm going to further explore are...	The curiosities this rewards are...
1	
2	
3	

What excites me about this is...	One small or big action I'm going to take on this path to deepen my experience is...

_____
_____
_____
_____
_____
_____
_____
_____
_____
_____
_____
_____
_____
_____
_____
_____
_____
_____
_____
_____

*"Change your life today.
Don't gamble on the future, act
now, without delay."*

———————————————

SIMONE DE BEAUVOIR

More on Sustainable Ambition

For resources that complement this book go to:
SustainableAmbition.com/curiosity

To work with Kathy Oneto, contact:
SustainableAmbition.com/contact

We love feedback!

We want to make sure we create value for you. If you
have feedback on how to make *My Little Book of Curiosity*
even better, please let us know! Contact us at
info@sustainableambition.com. We'd be very grateful.

Stay connected!

Learn more at: SustainableAmbition.com

Sign up for the newsletter at:
SustainableAmbition.com/subscribe

Listen to The Sustainable Ambition Podcast on your fa-
vorite podcast player.

About Sustainable Ambition

Sustainable Ambition offers a strategic approach to life+work integration. It is about crafting a fulfilling career to support your life from decade to decade. The end goal—experience more fulfillment in your professional and personal life with more ease, while still being ambitious.

In that description, you might pick up on the fact that Sustainable Ambition has two parts. The first is managing a career over time. The second is managing life+work in the current moment.

My Little Book of Curiosity is meant to support the first, navigating one's work over time and building a regenerative career by always staying curious and exploring what might be next.

About the Author

Kathy Oneto is a strategy executive and life+work and executive coach who bridges her two worlds, bringing strategic thinking to life+work planning and management. She is the founder of Sustainable Ambition and host of The Sustainable Ambition Podcast. Her mission is to help people attain more joy, satisfaction, and fulfillment in their careers from decade to decade, helping them to be ambitious with more ease and without burnout. She holds an MBA from Berkeley's Haas School of Business and a B.S. in Commerce from the University of Virginia. Kathy lives in San Francisco with her husband and the fog.

www.ingramcontent.com/pod-product-compliance
Lightning Source LLC
Chambersburg PA
CBHW020329130626
46549CB00003B/1091